HUFF and PUFF on
GROUNDHOG DAY

D1518805

TOTLINE® BOOKS
Warren Publishing House

Published by Totline® Publications
Editorial Office: PO Box 2250
                  Everett, WA 98203
Business Office: 23740 Hawthorne Blvd.
                  Torrance, CA 90505
Printed in Hong Kong through Phoenix Offset.
First Edition   10 9 8 7 6 5 4 3 2

Library of Congress Cataloging-in-Publication Data

Warren, Jean, 1940-
    Huff and Puff on Groundhog Day / by Jean Warren ; illustrated by Molly Piper;
    activity illustrations by Marion Hopping Ekberg. —1st ed.
        p.   cm. — (A totline teaching tale)
    Summary: Huff and Puff cover the sun so that a groundhog can come out and
enjoy an early spring day without worrying about seeing its shadow. Includes
related songs and activities.

    ISBN 1-57029-059-8 (hardcover) : $5.95

    (1. Groundhog Day—Fiction. 2. Woodchuck—Fiction. 3. Clouds—Fiction. 4. Shad-
ows—Fiction. 5. Handicraft. 6. Stories in rhyme.) I. Piper, Molly, 1949- ill. II. Ekberg,
Marion Hopping, ill. III. Title. IV. Series.
PZ8.3.W2459Ht   1995
(E)—dc20
                                                                    94-45662
                                                                    CIP
                                                                    AC

Totline Publications would like to acknowledge the following activity contributors:
Nancy Nason Biddinger, Orlando, FL
Susan Shroyer, Greensboro, NC
Diane Thom, Maple Valley, WA

HUFF and PUFF on GROUNDHOG DAY

By Jean Warren

Illustrated by Molly Piper
Activity Illustrations by Marion Hopping Ekberg

Huff and Puff
One winter's day
Floated past
Where groundhogs stay.

They saw a hole
And peeked inside.
"Look! A groundhog!"
They both cried.

The groundhog knew
That it was time
To begin
Her yearly climb.

Up, up she went,
Up to the top.
But suddenly
She had to stop.

Sweet
Dreams

"Oh, dear me,"
  She started to cry.
"I see the sun
  Up in the sky.

"Boo, hoo, hoo
  What can I do?
If I go out,
  My shadow will too!"

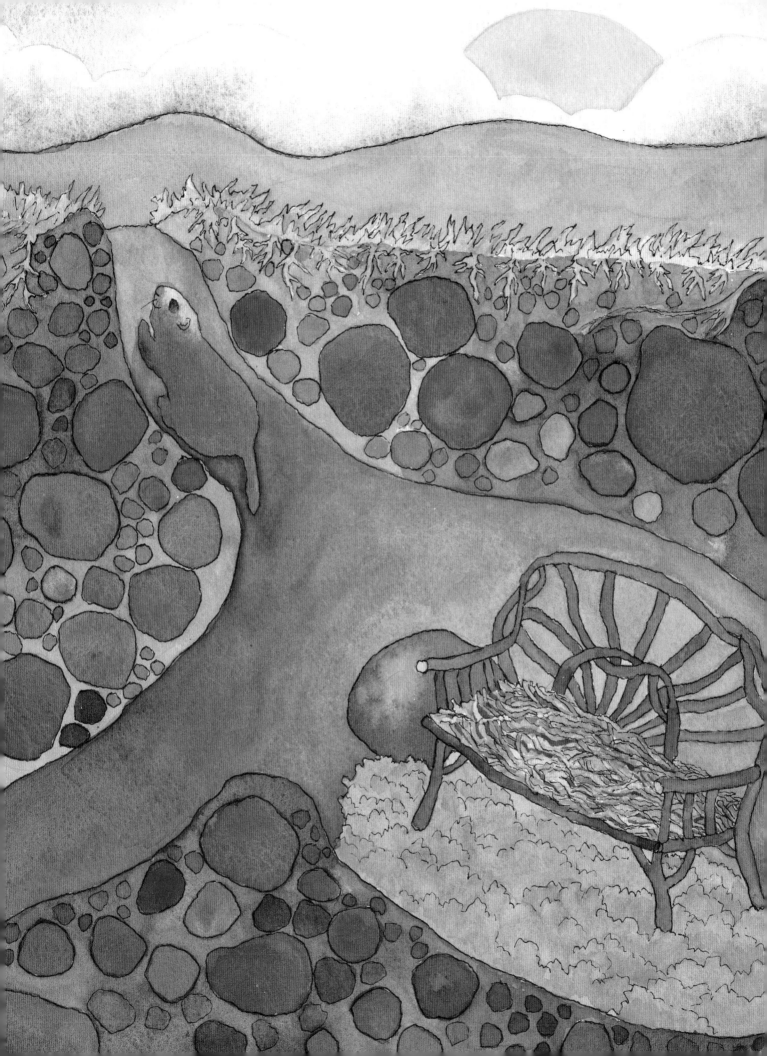

Huff and Puff
Heard her cry,
Then linked their arms
And flew up high.

They called their friends
To join the fun,
And soon they
Covered up the sun.

The groundhog saw
The sun disappear
And knew she now
Had nothing to fear.

So out she popped,
This time to play.
Now she knew
That she could stay.

The ground was hard,
The day was cold,
But she was happy
And she was bold.

She ran and ran
All around,
Enjoying every
Sight and sound.

She saw the early
Signs of spring—
Crocuses
And buds and things.

Huff and Puff
Heard her sigh,
"I have such good friends
In the sky.

Thank you for
My early fling,
Thank you for
This lovely spring!"

A Note to Parents and Teachers

The activities in this book have been written so that children in first, second, and third grade can follow most of the directions with minimal adult help. The activities are also appropriate for 3- to 5-year-old children, who can easily follow the steps with your help.

You may wish to extend the learning opportunities in this book by discussing shadows with your children. Encourage your children to discover what causes shadows by helping them create their own shadows. Make shadows on a wall and have your children identify objects by their shapes. Have your children make their own shadows on a wall. Discuss how shadows can appear to be larger on the wall than the objects that cause them. Another learning opportunity for your children is to stress position words such as up and down, in and out, high and low, and all around. Go back and retell the story in your own words, stressing these position words.

Children have always been fascinated by the story of the groundhog. Encourage your children to act out the story or just pretend to be groundhogs popping up and down out of a box. To extend this experience even further, let them decorate the inside of their box as their groundhog home.

All Huff and Puff stories lead naturally into discussions that can stretch children's imaginations as they visualize Huff and Puff's formations and accompany them on their adventures.

Groundhog Day Fun

SIGN LANGUAGE FUN

*Follow the directions below to learn to sign the words "little"
and "groundhog," and then sign the phrase "little groundhog"
whenever it appears in the songs on pages 21, 22, and 23.*

Little

Point both of your index
fingers away from your body
with your palms facing each
other and your thumbs up.
Move your palms slightly
toward each other.

Groundhog

Extend both of your index
fingers and thumbs with your
palms facing each other.
Place your fingertips on your
cheeks and pull back twice
to indicate whiskers.

Huff and Puff Flew Over the Meadow

Sung to: "The Bear Went Over the Mountain"

Huff and Puff flew over the meadow,
Huff and Puff flew over the meadow,
Huff and Puff flew over the meadow
One sunny winter's day.

They saw a little groundhog,
They saw a little groundhog,
They saw a little groundhog
Ready to come out and play.

"Oh, no! She'll see her shadow!
Oh, no! She'll see her shadow!
Oh, no! She'll see her shadow!
And then she cannot stay."

Huff and Puff called all their friends,
Huff and Puff called all their friends,
Huff and Puff called all their friends
And got in the sun's way.

The groundhog came out slowly,
The groundhog came out slowly,
The groundhog came out slowly,
Then knew she could stay.

Spring was coming early,
Spring was coming early,
Spring was coming early
And the groundhog now could play.

Huff and Puff flew over the meadow,
Huff and Puff flew over the meadow,
Huff and Puff flew over the meadow,
Then floated on their way.

Jean Warren

Little Groundhog
Sung to: "Twinkle, Twinkle, Little Star"

Little groundhog in your hole,

Is it winter, do you know?

If your shadow chases you,

That means winter is not through.

If your shadow can't be seen,

Spring is coming, new and green.

Diane Thom

Here's a Little Groundhog
Sung to: "I'm a Little Teapot"

Here's a little groundhog, furry and
    brown.

She's coming up to look around.

If she sees her shadow, down she'll go,

Then six more weeks of winter. Oh, no!

Nancy Nason Biddinger

Little Groundhog
Sung to: "Little White Duck"

There's a little groundhog
Who lives down in the ground,
A little groundhog
Who likes to look around.
She comes outside on Groundhog
   Day,
If she sees her shadow then she runs
   away.
There's a little groundhog
Who loves to stay and play
When spring's on its way.

Jean Warren

Can You Play?
Sung to: "Frere Jacques"

Little groundhog, little groundhog,
Can you play, can you play?
Popping up your head,
Popping up your head,
Can you play? Don't run away.

Little groundhog, little groundhog,
Can you play, can you play?
Running all around
On the cold, hard ground,
Can you play? Please, please stay!

Little groundhog, little groundhog,
Can you play, can you play?
You can't see your shadow,
You can't see your shadow,
Here comes spring, hip hurray!

Jean Warren

GROUNDHOG PUPPET

Make a groundhog that can go in and out of its hole!

1.

2.

3.

YOU WILL NEED
- felt-tip markers
- craft stick
- scissors
- small paper cup

1. Use felt-tip markers to draw a groundhog face on one end of a craft stick.

2. Carefully use scissors to cut a slit a little wider than the craft stick in the bottom of a paper cup.

3. Holding the paper cup upright, push the bottom of your craft stick through the slit in the paper cup.

4. Use the bottom of the craft stick to move the groundhog up and down to make her appear and disappear.

FOR MORE FUN
- Use a plastic-foam ball and a drinking straw to make a different paper-cup groundhog puppet. Push the straw into the ball and use glue to keep it in place. Draw a groundhog face on the ball. Poke a hole in the bottom of a paper cup and place the straw through the hole. Use the bottom half of the straw to move the groundhog up and down.

SHADOW PUPPET

Have a shadow show on your wall!

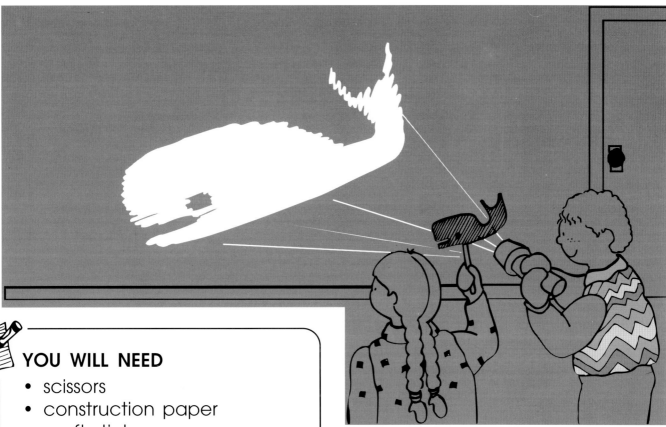

YOU WILL NEED

- scissors
- construction paper
- craft stick
- tape
- flashlight

1. Use scissors to cut an animal shape out of construction paper.

2. Attach the shape to a craft stick with tape.

3. Hold up a flashlight so that it shines on a wall. Then hold your animal shape in front of the light and watch the shadows that appear on the wall.

4. Move your animal shape closer to the light for larger shadows on the wall, and farther away for smaller shadows.

FOR MORE FUN

- Make several different animal shapes and act out a play on your wall. You could make characters to a story you already know, or make up your own play to act out.

SHADOW SHAPES

Make your hands into all different kinds of shadow creatures and characters. You can have your shadow show outside on a sunny wall when the sun is low in the sky, or you can shine a flashlight or a lamp on a wall in a darkened room in your home. Get your friends and family to make some shadows, too!

Snake

Butterfly

Crocodile

Rabbit

Dog

FOR MORE FUN

• Make light shapes by using scissors to cut different shapes, such as a circle, a square, or a heart, out of heavy paper. Turn off the lights in a room and shine a flashlight through the paper with the shape cut from it so that the light shines on a nearby wall.

SHADOW ART

Turn outdoor shadows into artwork!

4.

1-3.

YOU WILL NEED

- shadows
- large piece of light-colored paper
- felt-tip markers or crayons

1. Find an interesting shadow outside or inside.

2. Place a piece of paper on the part of the ground or floor where the shadow appears.

3. Use a felt-tip marker or a crayon to trace around the outline of the shadow.

4. Turn the paper in a different direction and trace around the shadow again. Your lines can overlap in designs.

5. Color in some of the spaces between the outlines to create unusual designs.

FOR MORE FUN

- Trace around large shadows such as a shadow of a bicycle. You can use a large piece of butcher paper on the ground.

- Gather some of your friends together and trace around each others' shadows on butcher paper.

SUN ART

Let the sun make shadow designs for you!

1–2.

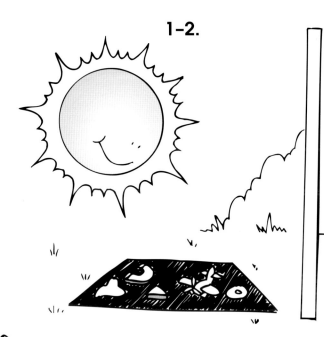

YOU WILL NEED

- small objects (rocks or toys work well)
- construction paper

1. Place small rocks or toys on a piece of construction paper.

2. Let the piece of paper sit outside in the sun for an afternoon.

3. Later on, pick up the objects and look for the outlines created by the sun. The sun will lighten the construction paper except in the places where you have placed the objects.

FOR MORE FUN

- Use a doily in the same way to create a lacy outline.

- Cut your own design out of a piece of paper, place it on a piece of construction paper, and let the sun shine on it for two or three hours.

WEATHER WHEEL
Keep track of the weather with this fun project!

YOU WILL NEED
- scissors
- posterboard
- felt-tip marker
- crayons
- brass paper fastener

1. Use scissors to cut a large circle out of a piece of posterboard.

2. Use a felt-tip marker to divide the circle into five sections, as if it were a pie.

3. Decorate each section with crayons to show a different kind of weather (sunny, cloudy, rainy, windy, and snowy).

4. Use scissors to cut an arrow shape out of posterboard.

5. Use scissors to poke a hole through the end of your arrow that is opposite the point. Then poke a hole through the center of the circle.

6. Insert a brass paper fastener through the hole in the arrow and then through the hole in the center of the circle.

7. Move the arrow each day so it points to the kind of weather for that day.

FOR MORE FUN
- Before you go to bed at night, try to guess what the weather for the next day will be. Point the arrow of your weather wheel toward that kind of weather. When you wake up, check to see if you guessed right. Move the arrow toward the real weather if you guessed wrong.

Adult supervision or assistance may be required.

SUNDIAL

Create your own special "clock" out of household items!

YOU WILL NEED

- scissors
- cardboard
- glue
- large, empty thread spool
- pencil
- felt-tip marker

1. Use scissors to cut a piece of cardboard into a circle about the size of a small pizza.

2. Glue a large empty spool to the middle of the cardboard circle.

3. Place a pencil in the hole in the middle of the spool, making sure it is standing straight up.

4. Take the sundial outside on a sunny day. Place it in a spot that will have sun shining on it all day.

5. Use a marker to mark the place on the cardboard where the pencil's shadow is. Make a note of what time it is.

6. Every hour, go out to see where the shadow has moved and make another mark on the cardboard for each hour.

7. At the end of the day, bring your sundial inside. What kind of pattern do the marks make?

FOR MORE FUN

- Decorate your sundial with bright, sunny colors or sun faces.

SHADOW TAG
Watch your shadow or you'll be It!

YOU WILL NEED
- a few friends
- a sunny day

1. Gather your friends and family together on a sunny day.

2. Choose one player to be It.

3. When It yells "Go!" all the players should start running and It should try to step on someone's shadow.

4. When It steps on a player's shadow, It should shout "Stop!"

5. All the players should stop running and the player whose shadow has been stepped on becomes It.

FOR MORE FUN
- If it's not a sunny day, do some shadow dancing inside. In a darkened room, shine a lamp or a large flashlight on a blank wall. You and your friends can wave, dance, twirl around, and even fall down, and watch how your shadow on the wall follows your every move. You could also try playing a shadow Simon Says game, where players look at the leader's shadow for directions.